WALKING in the LIGHT at MIDNIGHT

Graeme and Julia Cann

STUDY GUIDE
Seven Sessions

Walking in the Light at Midnight Study Guide © Copyright: Graeme & Julia Cann, 2025

All rights reserved. No part of this publication may be reproduced, stored in a retrieval system or transmitted in any form by any means, electronic, mechanical, photocopying, recording or otherwise, without the prior permission of the author — except in the case of brief quotation embodied in critical review and certain other non-commercial uses permitted by copyright law.

Walking in the Light at Midnight Study Guide

1. Suffering 2. Forgiveness. 3. Emotional Healing. I. Title.

ISBN: 978-1-7641117-2-0

All scripture references (unless specified) from the New Living Translation (NLT) © 2004, 2007, 2013, 2015. Used with permission.

PUBLISHED BY GRAEME CANN

www.graemecann.com

CONTENTS

INTRODUCTION 5

LEADERS NOTES 7

WEEK ONE 11

    Study One 12

WEEK TWO 15

    Study Two 16

WEEK THREE 19

    Study Three 20

WEEK FOUR 23

    Study Four 24

WEEK FIVE 27

    Study 28

WEEK SIX 31

    Study Six 32

WEEK SEVEN 35

    Study Seven 36

INTRODUCTION

Welcome to the study guide for *Walking in the Light at Midnight*.

Our sincere prayer is that as you read the book and participate in the group study, the thoughts, stories and scriptures we share might encourage you to ask the right questions and find helpful and encouraging answers.

Walking in the Light at Midnight is written with the goal of taking readers on a journey through the complexities of human emotions and the resilience of men and women of faith.

During your times together with your group you will encounter thought-provoking questions and insights that will enhance your understanding and appreciation of the issues of suffering, and the quest to find meaning, hope and peace amid your times of need. You will also have the opportunity to tell your own stories and strengthen and encourage the members of your group.

LEADER'S NOTES

*T*hank you for your ministry as a leader or facilitator of your small group. Our prayer is that the study around *'faith amid suffering'* will richly bless and encourage you all.

It is important that you read the book through first and that you encourage your group members to do the same. In the week prior to your meeting, it would be good to read the one or two chapters indicated in this study guide.

The primary principles of the book are:
1. *Pain and suffering are inevitable.*
2. *God does not cause people to suffer.*
3. *God presences Himself with us.*
4. *God uses pain and suffering to enrich our lives.*
5. *We do not choose our pathway through life, but we can choose how we walk it.*

*Y*ou might choose to have the group read one or two of the stories in each study. This is of course optional. However, it is important to read and contemplate the scripture passages together.

During each session people will undoubtedly have personal stories to share and it is important to allow time and space to facilitate that.

There is a personal diary page at the end of each study. Encourage each group member to write their thoughts after each meeting.

WEEK ONE

STUDY #1

based on

INTRODUCTION and

Chapter One

of

Walking in the Light at Midnight

STUDY #1

Graced with His presence

*T*oday we begin our study by reviewing the Introduction and the first chapter of *Walking in the Light at Midnight*. The verses that inspired the book are:

>Isaiah 43:2-3 and 5
>
>Psalm 23:4.
>
>Read these verses and discuss.

KEY QUESTIONS:

'*I*f living in the light means being a recipient and a reflector of all the love, grace and hope we receive from God, how do we do that when the heavens seem to be silent, God is a distant presence, and we are shrouded in a cloud of despair?'

What role does faith play in times of suffering?

*I*n the first chapter of the book Dawn and Ian describe their journey when the unthinkable happened to them. As a group re-read their story.

Now read and discuss each of the verses listed below:

Hebrews 13:5-6.
Isaiah 43: 1b-2.
Psalm 116:15.
Ephesians Chapter 1.

FOR FURTHER REFLECTION:

Consider this statement:
> 'I have learnt that life can be painful and that the Lord has not promised that every experience will be positive and pain free.'

Has this been your experience?

*W*hat has been the ways that God has encouraged you during difficult times?

Personal Diary Page

WEEK TWO
STUDY #2

based on

Chapters 2 & 3

of

Walking in the Light at Midnight

STUDY #2
The Light overcomes the darkness

*R*ead and review chapters 2 and 3 of *Walking in the Light at Midnight.*

KEY SCRIPTURES:
Psalms 145 and 34
1 John 4:15 -18
1 Peter 1:5-7
Romans 8:15-17

KEY TRUTH:
'*W*e have been inspired by the lives and ministry of those who emerged from the darkest nights and become untiring messengers of comfort and hope to others.'

REFLECT ON:
- James 1:2-3; 5 (page 13)
- Julias story (chapter 2. pages 16-21)
- Fanny Crosby's Story (pages 25-26)
- Nick Vujicic's story (pages 26-27)
- Wyley's Story (pages 27-29)

Question:

Why do you think Psalm 34 was such a help to both Julia and Wyley?

How have you dealt with fear in the past? How did God help you then?

Discussion.

Read Romans 8: 31-39. Which of these verses speaks to you personally? How do these specifically help you in times of hardship?

Personal Diary Page

WEEK THREE

STUDY #3

based on

Chapter 4

of

Walking in the Light at Midnight

STUDY #3
Love and Community

KEY SCRIPTURES:

Psalm 26: 1-3

Psalm 145

2 Corinthians 12:9

Matthew 11:28

Psalm 3:5

Ephesians 3:20

KEY THOUGHT:

The importance of love and community in times of hardship.

STATEMENT FOR REFLECTION:

'The Key to Vern and Elva's ability to walk through their valley was a firm belief that God was working out His purposes for them through this painful circumstance.

Read and review chapter 4 of "Walking in the light at Midnight.

In Vern and Elva's story pages 36-44, they speak about being supported by God's people and sustained by God's word.

One of the important parts of Vern and Elvas story was the support they received from their church and the Shepparton Church. What do we learn from this about the Church being the Body of Christ.

Discuss each of the Scriptures which they highlighted and share what they mean to you.

- Jeremiah 29-11-13
- Proverbs 19:21
- 2 Corinthians 12.9
- Matthew 11:28
- Ephesians 3:20

Personal Diary Page

WEEK FOUR
STUDY #4

based on

Chapter 5

of

Walking in the Light at Midnight

STUDY #4
God's Faithfulness And Our Restoration

KEY SCRIPTURES:

Psalm 56:8-13.
Ephesians 4:30-32.
Colossians 3:12-17.
1 Corinthians 13:12
2 Corinthians 13:11
Matthew 7:8

KEY TRUTH:

'God has an order, or if you like, a rhythm. It is about receiving His unfailing love and His unconditional forgiveness, allowing them to transform our minds and then loving and forgiving all others as He has loved and forgiven us. That's the rhythm. Freely receive, freely give.

Read and Review Chapter Five of Walking in the Light at Midnight (pages 47-58).

In this remarkable story shared by our friend, she believed from a very young age that despite her traumatic childhood, God loved her and had a wonderful plan for her life. This conviction is expressed in the psalm on page forty- five. Read this psalm together as a group. Pause at the end of each stanza and reflect.

What does it mean that ... *'God keeps track of all our sorrows.'?* Discuss.

'He has collected all our tears in His bottle and recorded each one in His book.' Discuss.

'My enemies will retreat when I call to Him for help, This I know! God is on my side!' Discuss.

'I praise the Lord for what He has promised.' Discuss.

'I trust in God, why should I be afraid. What can mere mortals do to me.' Discuss.

'I will fulfill my vows to you, O God, and will offer a sacrifice of thanks for your help.' Discuss.

'You have rescued me from death; you have kept my feet from slipping. So now, I can walk in your presence, O God, in your life-giving light.' Psalm 56: 8-13. Discuss.

Personal Diary Page

WEEK FIVE
STUDY #5

based on

Chapter 6

of

Walking in the Light at Midnight

STUDY #5
A Radical Truth — A Radical Gift

KEY SCRIPTURES:

Psalm 139: 1-6
Psalm 139:7-12
Psalm 139: 13-16

KEY THOUGHT:

'In times of trial God comes to us down the pathway of our thankfulness bearing the gift of revelation.'

Read and review chapter 6 of Walking in the Light at Midnight.

Read Psalm 139: 1-6 together.

What knowledge is too wonderful for David to understand?

What has God revealed to you through your trials that you found at the time too wonderful to understand?

Read Psalm 139: 7-12 together.

*D*avid now understands that God is always pursuing him, not out of obligation but because of His unfailing love.

Have you experienced this truth? What helped you to understand it?

Read Psalm 139: 13-18.

These may be the most powerful words ever written to Christ-followers. Do you agree?

What makes them so powerful?

Personal Diary Page

WEEK SIX
STUDY #6

based on

Chapter 7

of

Walking in the Light at Midnight

STUDY #6
The Power of Forgiveness

*R*ead and review chapter seven of Walking in the Light at Midnight.

KEY SCRIPTURES:
Matthew 6: 9-15.
Ephesians 4:30-32

KEY TRUTH:

*T*ake time to reflect on whether your well-being is impacted by unforgiveness. Resentment is a strong emotion that cannot be resolved by being pushed down into our subconscious. Most of us in our lifetime have had valid reasons for feeling resentful, but its validity does not neutralise its toxicity.

Read Ephesians 4: 25-32 together.

***Five Steps to Forgiving** another. Discuss each of these steps using the material in the book as a resource.

1. Identify who is to blame for the hurtful event, and who is responsible for the response you have made to the event.
2. Own the resentment and bitterness. How have they caused harm in your life and hurt to the people you love.
3. Ask those you have hurt to forgive you.
4. Forgive the person who hurt you "as God in Christ has forgiven you.
5. Turn your tombstones into milestones.

* **NOTE**: We strongly recommend that you read our book: 'FORGIVENESS! THE KEY TO EMOTIONAL FREEDOM' for detailed more information on these Five Steps.

Personal Diary Page

WEEK SEVEN

STUDY #7

based on

Chapter 8 & 9

of

Walking in the Light at Midnight

STUDY #7
Resilience and Hope

KEY SCRIPTURES:

Psalm 42

Psalm 51.

John 3: 16:21

Matthew 25; 24-40.

Romans 8: 31-39

KEY TRUTH:

*T*ry to imagine what it meant for an immortal God with unlimited power and majesty to assume human form, laying down all His divine privileges and coming as a slave, to suffer and die for the entire world.

Read and review chapters eight and nine.

*R*esilience, is our ability to adapt to and find purpose and meaning even when passing through a time of trial. Our resilience comes from a deep conviction that someone far greater, more loving and mor powerful is in control. Discuss.

*H*ope is the capacity to see beyond a trial or a handicap and know that I have something that no person or circumstance can take away. That is the love, presence and grace of God my Father, the Salvation that come through Christ and the presence of the Holy Spirit. Discuss.

Read the following Scriptures and share with each other how they speak into hope and resilience

Psalm 51:1-11;

Psalm 51: 12-15.

*A*s this is our final study share any insights you have gained and decisions you may have made during this series. Pray for each other.

Personal Diary Page

www.ingramcontent.com/pod-product-compliance
Lightning Source LLC
Chambersburg PA
CBHW061732070526
44583CB00024B/3108